MW00652446

SEMIOTEXT(E) INTERVENTION SERIES

© 2020 Bollati Boringhieri editore, Torino. Originally published as *Virus sovrano? L'asfissia capitalistica* by Donatella Di Cesare.

Published by Semiotext(e)
PO BOX 629, South Pasadena, CA 91031
www.semiotexte.com

Design: Hedi El Kholti

ISBN: 978-1-63590-148-1
Distributed by the MIT Press, Cambridge, Mass.,
and London, England
Printed in the United States of America

Donatella Di Cesare

Immunodemocracy

Capitalist Asphyxia

Translated by David Broder

semiotext(e)
intervention
series □ 30

Contents

1

THE COMING ILLS

It had already been in the air for some time. Many pressed on with their lives, preferring to ignore it— whether out of incredulity, suspicions they harbored, or mere resignation. But then everything was shut down—like when a well-worn mechanism that has been whirring for too long finally grinds to a halt. A spectral silence descended, pierced by the high-pitched wailing of the sirens.

Despite the sunny colors that tinted the streets of Rome in spring of 2020, everything was pervaded by a gloomy stupor. The tables disappeared from outside the bars and the students' voices vanished, too. Half-empty buses raced down roads that had now fallen all but silent—discordant notes, and a trace of the febrile world that had gone before.

From one window to the next, everyone peered at their neighbors. Down on the pavement, two acquaintances would head toward each other as if driven by some spontaneous impetus. But then the greeting would turn into a pained gesture, advising against it—a request for the other to keep their distance.

After centuries of history, the eternal city was holding its breath, in a stunned apnea, an anguished wait.

This epochal event marks a watershed. It has already changed the twenty-first century—and even our way of seeing it. Amidst the ambient disorientation and disconcertment, many have repeated one same word: "unprecedented." This label is quite rightly applied to the global pandemic unleashed by the coronavirus. It is well-known that an event is never a *unicum*, if only because it takes up a place within the plot of history. Yet in this case, comparisons with past happenings— even recent ones—are jarring, discordant. The twentieth century suddenly seems to have become remote, like it never had been before. Hence why anyone who uses twentieth-century lenses to decipher what's going on risks quickly running into trouble.

One might easily think back to a shock closer to our own time, to 9/11. The comparison has been made before. The new millennium began in 2001 with the collapse of the Twin Towers, a terrorist act followed live around the world. Yet there are glaring differences with today's situation. Even insofar as 9/11 was the first global event—and for many it really was a shocking tragedy—it was nonetheless viewed from afar, through the filter of the TV screen. Ethical questions were raised over "other people's pain" and the much-spectacularized images from that day; there were long debates on the political questions raised by the "war on terror" and the incipient state of emergency. Yet the towers' collapse did not really derail the onward march of history, the succession of decades from the postwar period to today. For its onward march remained dominated by confidence in progress— and destined to ever-greater wellbeing.

Invisible, impalpable, ethereal, almost abstract, the coronavirus attacks our bodies. We are no longer just spectators—rather, we are the victims. No one can save themselves. The attack has taken hold in the air itself. The virus slyly targets the respiratory system, taking the breath of life away and bringing a horrible death. It is the virus of asphyxia.

The coming ill is a murderous biological virus, a catastrophic germ. But this time, it isn't a metaphor. And what gets ill is the physical body— the exhausted body of humanity, the fatigued nervous organism. For years already, it has been subjected to an intolerable tension, to an extreme agitation, to the point of apnea. Perhaps it is no accident that the virus proliferates in the respiratory tracts, through which the breath of life passes. The body is torn away from a life running at an accelerated pace. It can no longer keep up. It gives in. It stops.

Is this the dreaded "accident of the future"? Any diagnosis on this score would be too hasty. But it is hard to believe that this is just a misfortune, a setback, a peripheral episode—and not rather more of a fatal event, ripping through the heart of the system. This is not just a crisis, but a slow-motion catastrophe. The virus has stopped the mechanism from functioning. What we are seeing, here, is a planetary convulsion, the spasm produced by a virulent fever. Acceleration as an end unto itself has inexorably reached the point of inertia. This is a tetanization of the world.

Everything seems to come to a halt, in a bitter contraction, a chain reaction, a viral effect. This is an internal malfunction, an unforeseen breakdown—although it had in fact been foreseeable for some time! The cogs are running on empty. One can almost hear the dissonance of the gears no longer working in harmony. Just as it is impossible to decipher the secret order in the depths of the catastrophe, it is difficult to say what this enigmatic suspension really means. Perhaps the virus is a final, dramatic alarm sign? Or perhaps our vital resistance is again being tested, before the ultimate collapse arrives?

The coronavirus has triggered an involution—and not a revolution, as some imagined. This is not to deny that this unexpected halt may also provide a pause for reflection, an interval before a fresh beginning. But it is clear that this is an irreversible development.

The desire for change which has been building up over recent years is impossible to ignore. It stems from a perverse, obsolete, unjust economic system—a system that produces hunger and social inequality, war and terror, worldwide climate collapse and the exhaustion of resources. But now the world is being shaken by a virus. This is not the event that was expected to pull the emergency brake on history, faced with the incessant storm that swirls over the ruins of progress.

The unforeseen virus has suspended the inevitable continuity of the always-the-same. It has interrupted a growth that had become an uncontrollable, measureless excrescence without end. And any crisis always contains the possibility of redemption. So, will the alarm be heeded? Will this violent pandemic also provide the opportunity for change? The coronavirus has torn bodies away from the whirring cogs of the economy. It is a tremendously deadly force, but also a vital one. For the first time, the crisis is extra-systemic; yet, it cannot be assumed that capital will prove unable to profit from this. If nothing will be as it was before, it is also possible that everything will be thrown into the most irrecoverable disrepair. The brake has been pulled already—what comes next is up to us.

2

BETWEEN CALCULATIONS AND PROGNOSIS: ON THE "END OF THE WORLD"

It seems that the epidemic was not, in fact, all that unforeseeable. Better, over the last five years there had been repeated warnings. And here I am not speaking of fiction or eschatological visions. Already in 2017, the WHO (World Health Organization) had warned that a pandemic was imminent—it was just a matter of time. This was no abstract hypothesis. In September of 2019, a team at the Global Preparedness Monitoring Board, made up of experts from the WHO and the World Bank, reported, "The threat of a pandemic spreading around the globe is a real one. A quick-moving pathogen has the potential to kill tens of millions of people, disrupt economies, and destabilize national security."

But how on earth did this alarm go so unnoticed? This is a question of science, even before it is a political one. We might suspect that academic capitalism is not such an aid to research. Interpretations are offered, indications provided, and possibilities outlined—but all these studies then gather dust in governmental libraries and ministerial bookshelves. Scientists' toil ends up being reduced to nothing more than an idle exercise in literary production.

Even the scientific findings that do get some hearing in the outside world risk being rendered ineffective, given the lack of collaborative efforts. An international treaty was set out under the auspices of the WHO back in 2005, but it has been neglected. Despite repeated WHO warnings, each state has stubbornly followed its own—often confused and slapdash—policy, suggesting that the virus is other people's problem. Some, like Trump and Bolsonaro, even denied the danger, and continued to do so for as long as they could.

The global epidemic unleashed by COVID-19 can be called the third great event of the twenty-first century. The terrorist attack of September 11, 2001 was followed by a second unforgettable event, the great financial and credit crisis of 2008. Triggered by a bubble in the real estate market, over subsequent years it produced a global recession and a boundless indebtedness, which proliferated through its own contagion mechanisms. There are many similarities between the financial crisis and the health crisis, and finance, too, has its viruses. But beyond the metaphors, COVID-19 is something that comes from the body; it seizes up the whirring cogs of capitalism from the outside. Nonetheless, there are convincing connections to be made between that conjuncture and this one. The one crisis points to the other, or better, foreshadows and prepares it, in a sort of uninterrupted chain of catastrophe.

The dawn of the third millennium is characterized by an enormous difficulty in imagining the future. We fear the worst. There is no longer expectation, or an opening to the future. Rather, the future seems closed: in the best-case scenario, it is destined to reproduce the past, reiterating it in a present that appears in the trappings of a future perfect.

It is no accident that surveys, predictions and conjectures are all proliferating at such an intensified rate. This should be seen as a sign of the desire to impose control on the "worst-case future"—to contain it by calculating it. This is the mark, the signature, of our era. Now, the times to come are a threat that looms over us in a troubled sky. The prevalent form of expectation is brimming with anxiety and heavy with apprehension.

For centuries, the world has been agitated by "the end"—a terrifying and unfathomable prospect. But today this "end" has a real significance. This is no longer only the "end of history"—that macabre neoliberal prophecy that has spent recent decades repeating that "there is no alternative" to the ruthless economy of capital. "The end of the world" is now taken as a self-evident fact, above all in the empirical sciences: climatology, geophysics, oceanography, biochemistry, ecology. But the countless references to it by philosophers and anthropologists should not go ignored, either. In their 2014 essay *The Ends of the World*, Déborah Danowski and Eduardo Viveiros de Castro investigated the fears of "the end." Two women, Isabelle Stengers and Donna Haraway, have especially discussed resistance in the "catastrophic times" to capitalist destruction, and survival on an "infected planet."

The philosopher Günther Anders called it the "last age"—the age of the end. He perhaps went further even than other philosophers in prophesying the extermination of humanity, as he issued a powerful warning against a suicide that seemed to be ineluctably standing out on the horizon. This was true even when he was writing in the immediate postwar era; and very little has changed since then.

The rush toward ecological disaster has not been halted, despite all the awareness-raising. It's just that we have turned from nuclear winter to global warming.

But one thing is new. For those of us who live in the third millennium, the imminent end is a historical fact—and it's no longer only cosmological in character. The historical certainty of the end sets its stamp on an era that takes form in an apocalyptic scenario lacking either theological resonance or political promise. The apocalypse takes shape in full modernity—indeed, a secular, scientific modernity. The coming ills make their entry in a moment when humanity was already racing to avoid its own self-destruction.

One idea today making headway holds that the death of the individual might coincide with the end of the world. And after that death nothing would be left behind—neither shared memory nor others' recollection, neither inheritance nor legacy. So, everything would have been in vain. What humanity has built up over the centuries and millennia would end forever, in an extermination which is much more than a simple extinction. In the many millenarianisms of the past, it was possible to fantasize about the end times, in the whirlwind of belief, expectation and delirium. We today are the first whose lot it is to believe in an end without a way out. The first whose lot it is to think that maybe we shall be the last.

The idea of progress has waned. But what is also disappearing is the confidence that it is possible to affect the course of events, avoid the inevitable and improve humanity's fate. It seems that there is no longer redemption, reparation or salvation. Hope seems condemned to remain a dead letter. There is no promise that present sufferings will be repaid by the advent of justice. Everything proves terribly irredeemable. Precisely because history loses its meaning, each existence becomes a history unto itself, dispersed and separated off into a singular, indecipherable destiny. The ties with other existences, with other individual stories, are cut. It thus becomes impossible to read one's own defeat as part of a History whose outcome is yet to be decided. It becomes impossible to see one's own life as a contribution to building another world—whether that means heavenly bliss or the earthly justice of a classless society. The legacy being passed along is a world getting worse, and the ancient pact between the generations is broken: the parents blame the children, and they in turn blame the parents.

This is the privatization of the future. It is a source of not only distress but also a diffuse violence.

A human life is confined to the stretch of its own physical existence alone, reduced to its own biography—and all its expectations are now focused within these limits. Hence the decisive importance that the body takes on—for this is the fight against the limit of death played out in full. As pain, illness and old age become absolutely intolerable, similarly pleasure, friendship, and love represent unique gifts salvaged from the grief of catastrophe—specific and discontinuous moments of a present utilized for one's own benefit, in a constant struggle against others. Each person cultivates their own individual utopia, a chimera formed of success, wealth and prestige. Most are doomed to crash up against the rocks. How can these rash promises be fulfilled? How can this narcissistic fantasizing be made to fit with reality? The privations and sacrifices are hard to bear, because they are not interpreted in a shared, historical perspective. So, they instead open the way for despondency, frustration and rage.

This is where the defeat of politics becomes fully apparent. Listless and concentrated on a tomorrowless present, politics bounces from one emergency to the next, attempting to keep up with events and ride the wave. Irresponsibility—a lack of answers for the future generations—seems to be this politics' most particular trait.

The disaster that has now been announced only feeds the sense of impotence. Is it already too late? All this alarm may be the expression—who knows?—of a premature catastrophism. Maybe science has a last-minute surprise in store? Perhaps. But the very functioning of techno-scientific society does not leave much space for illusions, with its standards of well-being and its canons of prosperity (unless, that is, it reviews them).

3

CAPITALIST ASPHYXIA

It has taken the arrival of a malicious virus to force a pause. It's impossible to avoid immediately thinking of a bizarre and tragic paradox. For a while we are stopping for breath, breathing a little, we do so only because of the imminent danger—because COVID-19, the asphyxiating virus, is threatening to take our breath away.

We don't know what the intense "pause" of "rest" means anymore. For us, it sits too close to the drowsiness of sleep or even to the eternal sleep of death. We do say "rest in peace," after all. Maybe this border with death is the reason why rest provokes such anxiety. The virus reminds us of this, too.

All of a sudden, breathing assumes a value it had never had before. Everywhere there is talk of respiration and oxygen. As the air in towns and cities grows less polluted, doctors and nurses in hospitals' intensive care units are every day fighting to ward off the deadly, irreparable asphyxia. After all that has happened, breathing should no longer be a given.

The slowdown-virus has got the better of acceleration. Only temporarily, it's to be hoped. The hiatus it has provoked does not have the colors of the fiesta but the grim and gloomy aspect of an epilogue. And yet in this forced standstill, the aberration of yesterday's frenzy—the agitation, the hyperactivity, the shortness of breath—is becoming apparent.

Temporal asphyxiation has been the dark ill of recent years. Inadequacy, anxiety and panic pervade existence. And existence is condemned to fear of the moment to come—a moment has already melted away even as it looms over us. It's not only that we are unable to stop: we are also incapable of dwelling in a time where we no longer find any shelter. Every moment is now uninhabitable.

Time seems to have been eaten up even before it has been granted to us. We are on an escalator descending ever more quickly—and we have to run up the steps to avoid the abyss. Improvised, fictitious escapes, private revolts and minor boycotts serve little purpose—and we often pay dearly for them. Oases of deceleration and slowdown strategies are nothing but palliatives.

In this era of advanced capitalism, no one can escape the dizzying economy of time. We are apparently free and sovereign. But taking a closer look, the growth imperative, the compulsion to produce and the obsession with productivity combine to ensure that freedom and coercion subtly end up coinciding. We are living in coercive freedom and in free coercion. That is the only way of coping with the challenge of everyday life, which leaves us exhausted and breathless. If at night we feel a vague sense of guilt, this is not because we have transgressed the laws of ethics or eluded religious commandments. Rather, it is because we have failed to keep pace and remain in step with the breakneck rhythm of a world running at high speed.

But this speed crashes to a standstill—and the acceleration ends in inertia. In this frantic stalemate situation, danger mounts. This is all the more true because, while the elites have internalized the rules of acceleration, workers find themselves bent to alienating rhythms and the unemployed are weighed down by exclusion. But the acceleration machine appears to have gotten totally out of control.

Slowdown, sabotage? How can we halt the mad rush without making the self-destructive leap? How can we stop the malign work of the cogs that are ruining our lives and leeching vampire-like on our time?

But, on closer inspection, the coming ill had in fact come already. One had to be blind not to see the catastrophe lurking around the corner, not to recognize the malign velocity of the capitalism now engulfing us in its devastating spiral, in its compulsive, asphyxial vortex.

4

OMNIPOTENCE AND VULNERABILITY

For the first time, an invisible and unknown being—an almost immaterial one—has paralyzed the whole of technologically advanced human civilization. This had never happened before—still less on this worldwide scale. Old dogmas have been turned to dust, ironclad certainties deeply shaken. Already, everything has changed: from economic axioms to geopolitical balances, forms of life and social realities.

But this epochal transformation has generated such anxiety because it is an outright reversal of perspective. Up till yesterday, we could consider ourselves omnipotent even as we marched through the ruins— the first, unique, even in our supreme capacity for destruction. But this supremacy has been taken from us by a power superior to our own—and more destructive. That this power should be a virus, such a tiny portion of organized matter, makes this an even more traumatic event.

Even the tiniest life-form can topple us from our throne, depose us, unseat us. Perhaps life on this planet will take new directions—who knows? For now, we must acknowledge that we are not as omnipotent as we had once presumed. Rather, we are extremely vulnerable.

Neither divine punishment nor the nemesis of history. It is difficult not to see the pandemic as the consequence of our devastating, short-sighted choices regarding the environment. We have treated planet Earth as a dumping ground, a warehouse for dross and garbage, a heap of ruins. Yet it is impossible to save the planet without transforming the world. Ecology itself must change: yet to free itself of patriarchal concepts, it must consider the Earth as the *oíkos*, the domestic sphere of life. There is a striking link between ecology and economy. The ecological collapse is the product of capitalism. The fusion between techno-economy and biosphere is plain for all to see—as are its deadly results. *Anthropocene* is the name that has been given to the geological era conditioned by human domination, in which nature has been irreparably eroded.

But this violent process would not have been possible if it were not for the burning flame of capital. That is why it is impossible to imagine a new way of inhabiting the earth, unless we bid farewell to the planetary debt economy.

Capitalist realism has absorbed every hotbed of resistance in the imagination, telling us that this system is the ultimate horizon. Walls have been erected and reinforced in the bid to conceal any other possibility. We have lived in the asphyxiating present of a windowless world, purporting to immunize itself from all that is outside, other and beyond. Closedness prevailed, and the immunitarian impulse won out—that is, the obstinate desire to remain intact, uncorrupted, beyond harm. Xenophobia—fear of the stranger—and exophobia—the bottomless fear of all that is external and comes from the outside—are the inevitable collateral damage. Here, the future is preempted, precisely in order to avoid the future. In this preventative policing regime, condemned to a protracted state of alarm and an infinite torpor, all possibility of change is exorcized in advance.

The pandemic sheds a spotlight on all this—and reveals the disease of identity. In the final pages of his book *Métamorphoses*, published at the start of 2020, Emanuele Coccia defined the virus as a transformative force. Because it freely circulates from one body to another, it contaminates and alters. It is impossible to avoid viral metamorphosis, unless we want to shield ourselves from life itself. We are not the same as we used to be; our flesh never stops changing. Each person bears the mark of other forms that life has pervaded and crossed through. In vain would anyone purport to avoid contamination.

While we could hardly defend the virus—or perhaps, speak on its behalf—it is worth considering its transformative capacity. It could even change the face of the planet—and for this very reason, it inspires alarm and fear. As Jean Baudrillard wrote some years ago, the virus is the "malign genius of alterity." In this sense, it is both the worst and the best of things, a lethal infection and a vital contagion. In its radical inhumanity, the virus is a wholly unknown other, which is nonetheless no different from us.

The virus is the extreme sign, the obscure symptom, of that disease of identity which emerges in such acute form in air-conditioned, purified settings, in sterilized spaces from which the other has been expelled. In these zones of artificial immunity, the self that sought to *inhabit* a space secured from the extraneous instead begins to devour itself.

The antibodies that ought to have defended it try to attack it. Mysterious pathologies, unmeasurable disturbances born of disinfection itself, then spread like wildfire. Superprotected and disarmed, the self discovers its tragic vulnerability. It is the absence of the other—its erasure—that secretes and brings on the incomprehensible alterity of the virus.

Nation states' wars against migrants, the immunitarian logic of exclusion, now appears in all its ridiculous crudeness. Nothing has been able to protect us from the coronavirus—not even the sovereigntists' patriotic walls or their arrogant and violent borders. The global pandemic shows the impossibility of saving ourselves, unless we turn to mutual aid.

That is why this event must inspire us to rethink how we inhabit the earth. Inhabiting is not a synonym for having or possessing, but rather for being and existing. It does not mean being rooted in the soil but, rather, breathing the air. This is something we had forgotten. To exist is to breathe. Existence is that which comes out, moves from its origin, migrates, inhales and exhales the world's breath, projects it outside of itself, immerses itself and re-emerges. In so doing, it participates in migration and the transformation of life. This does not mean drifting off into the cosmos. The breath that comes and goes, that rhythmic movement that sets the beat for our being in the world, suggests that we are all strangers, temporary guests, migrants pushed back and forth between each other, resident foreigners.

The virus struck at our breathing, after the disease of identity had already been apparent for some time. It has stripped away the veil that had previously hidden our vulnerability. Suddenly, we discovered that we are exposed: that we are not impermeable, resistant, immune. Yet to be vulnerable is not to be missing something. Judith Butler has rightly invited us to interpret vulnerability as a resource. She has pointed to our grief faced with the death of others as the experience that deeply unsettles and disconcerts the sovereign ego. Perhaps the loss of the other—collective grief—is the basis for designing a new politics of vulnerability.

5

STATE OF EXCEPTION AND SOVEREIGN VIRUS

The coronavirus is so-called because of the characteristic crown in which it is garlanded. This crown
is evocative and terrifying—it is powerful. Hence,
even the virus's name tells us that it is sovereign. It
escapes and eludes, it transgresses borders, it con-
quers. The coronavirus makes a mockery of that
sovereignty which purports either to ignore it—an
absurd pretense, if ever there was one—or else to
draw some advantage from it. And it becomes the
name of an ungovernable catastrophe that has
everywhere unmasked the limits of a political
governance reduced to technocratic administration.
For as we know, capitalism is no natural disaster.

When we speak of a "state of exception," we are
thinking of the way this formula was theorized by
Giorgio Agamben in his famous 1995 book *Homo
Sacer: Sovereign Power and Bare Life*. The publication

of Agamben's book would change both the terms of political philosophy and its concepts. The exception is a paradigm of government even in post-totalitarian democracy. Therefore, this democracy maintains a troubling connection with the past. Indeed, we need to reckon with all the measures taken in the name of emergency—that is, with the decrees that were meant to be exceptional but have instead become the norm. Executive power abuses legislative and judicial power; parliament is ever more divested of its functions. It is difficult not to agree with this vision, which now provides the outlines of everyday political practice.

As Agamben articulated his own position, he again took up the words of the controversial German jurist Carl Schmitt, asserting that "sovereign is he who decides on the exception." But he also reworked the theses of Michel Foucault and Hannah Arendt. Both had, in their different ways, reflected on how lives are governed in a liberal democracy.

Today, opinions diverge more than ever before. There is a very widespread—sometimes unconscious—neoliberalism which sees present-day democracy as the panacea for all evils, as synonymous with public debate. Others take a highly critical view, considering this as a hollowed-out democracy, ever more formal and ever less political. This is expressed in a governance mechanism that proceeds by way of decree, and news reporting that sublimates the people in "public opinion."

To speak of a "state of exception" is not to think that democracy is the antechamber of dictatorship or that the premier is a tyrant. Rather, it means that we need to recognize for the umpteenth time, again faced with the pandemic, the legislation by decree that has suspended democratic freedoms.

Reduced to its crude, extreme synthesis, sovereign power is the right to dispose of others' lives—even to the point of having them killed. But the "sovereign" discussed today is not the monarch of times past. He is not the tyrant who put people to death on the scaffold, wielding brutal violence and issuing blatantly arbitrary decisions. Yet, the figure of the sovereign exception does persist even in modern regimes. It's just that it operates in the background, becoming ever less readable and sinking into the depths of administrative practice. This does not mean that it has lost its political importance. The agent of this power is the subaltern functionary, the bureaucrat today on duty, the stubborn guard corps. In short: however unspeakable it may be, the democratic institutions do rely on the sovereign exception. The old power continues to operate in the interstices and shadow zones of the rule-of-law state.

The monster dozes away within the administrative machine. Which is to say, the same administrative machine which did not buy respirators for the intensive care wards in time—and coolly left "the oldest" exposed and let them die—through its derelictions of duty, its cynicism and its incompetence. But we could mention countless such examples. From the migrants drowned at sea or handed over for torture by zealous Libyan guards, to the homeless people abandoned along the sides of the streets, to the prisoners who die of methadone overdoses after revolts on the wing. No citizen ever thinks that his turn could come, too.

The "state of exception" paradigm remains valid, even if in many regards it appears a twentieth-century matter. If one were to level a critique against Agamben, it would surely revolve around the ever more intricate character of modern power—a sovereignty that is anything but monolithic. For sovereign right is exercised through containment and exclusion, through a complex and dynamic mechanism. It is no accident that states delegitimize one another. What counts is immunity: the sovereign is he who protects from the diffuse conflict raging on the outside. He bio-contains, he safeguards. And he does so as part of that famous clash which dominates the Western narration. In this clash, the progressive spaces of democratization—which the immune have the right to inhabit—are set against the barbaric peripheries where all the others can be exposed. In this fairy tale, there is no mention of the police violence that post-totalitarian, legitimate sovereignty exercises against "others." The dangers bearing down on the immune and the supposedly immunized also go overlooked.

Today, biopower is always also a psychopower: the one crosses over to the other. This is well-illustrated by techno-sanitary procedures, and indeed by the dominant status enjoyed by biotechnology. Those who foment securitarian passions play with the fire of fear—and will end up getting burned by it. Everything gets out of hand. This follows the same pattern as technology: those who use it are used by it; those who command it are in turn deposed by it. The political-administrative governance that governs in the name of exception is itself governed by that which proves ungovernable. This continual role reversal is a striking aspect of the current situation.

6

IMMUNITARIAN DEMOCRACY

In Las Vegas, homeless people were lined up like cars on the floor of an open-air parking lot. The city's over-one-hundred hotels had been closed due to the emergency—but even so, their rooms were reserved for those who had money. Left with nowhere to stay after contagion broke out at the Catholic Charities, where they had previously found shelter, the homeless were lined up on the ground at a secure distance from one another, each laid within a white rectangle painted on the cement. A few disabled people lay on the asphalt alongside their wheelchairs. The photos were chilling. The virus cast an unsparing spotlight on social apartheid.

Lesbos and Moria—the despicable gates of Europe, where refugees are massed together in tents and makeshift shelters. This is what's called administrative detention: and though they have committed no crime, these people are enclosed behind barriers and barbed wire. This is a police management of migration. Cold, hunger, overcrowding, a lack of water: the unhygienic, unsanitary conditions are ideal terrain for the epidemic to spread. But the warning signs raised by humanitarian organizations were not heeded. European public opinion had other things to worry about. In essence, nation states' war against migrants—indulged and supported by their own citizens, proud and jealous of their rights—could continue undisturbed, indeed now with a few extra allies.

In India, Prime Minister Narendra Modi decreed the lockdown overnight without any warning. The first to be hit were internal migrants, in their hundreds of thousands. Now left without either a job or a home, they tried to jump onto any still-available means of transportation in order to return from the megacities to the rural areas from where they had first hailed. But the shutdown was already in force. Some self-isolated in the trees, with neither medicine nor food. Others walked miles upon miles by foot—a desperate flight, captured and narrated by social media, TV channels and newspapers. The other victims, as well as migrants, were the dalits—the lowest of the low, those without any caste standing, the oppressed who used to be called "untouchables" because they were associated with impure activities, and thus the object of discrimination.

The poor and rejected do not inspire compassion: rather, they draw a mix of anger, disapproval and fear. The poor person is not worthy of redemption, for they are a failed consumer, a minus and not a plus on the unyielding balance-sheet, just as the rejected are a mere useless black hole. All responsibility for their fate is dropped in advance; any charity toward them a commendable initiative.

The cordon sanitaire *of neglect risks widening beyond all proportion. The disparity between the protected and the defenseless, which defies any idea of justice, has never been as striking, as barefaced, as in the crisis the coronavirus has prompted.*

It is difficult to understand what is happening unless we look back—even amidst these conditions of shock and upheaval—to the recent past. The virus has sharpened and intensified an already established situation which has suddenly appeared in all its darkest and most heinous aspects. Seen through the prism of the virus, democracy in the Western countries has turned out to be a system of immunity that had already been operating for some time. Now, it is merely doing so in less concealed fashion.

Debates on democracy examine how it can be defended, reformed, and improved. But what they do not put into doubt are its borders, what it means to belong to a democracy, or—still less— the bind that holds it together: namely, the fear of contagion, the fear of the other, the terror at what lies outside of it. This means overlooking the reality that discrimination is always-already there, latent and concealed. Even those citizens who do fight against racism (a very powerful virus!)—for instance, by demanding the opening of their country's borders—take for granted their "ownership" over their "own" country, which is to say, their national belonging.

There is thus a presupposition at work, here— that of a closed natural community prepared to safeguard its own sovereign integrity. This potent fiction, which has been dominant for centuries, has driven the belief that birth—in the guise of a "signature"—is a sufficient basis for national belonging. Even if globalization has loosened such connections, the political perspective does not seem to have changed any great deal. The discussion focuses on matters of internal administration: reforming laws, improving efficiency, modernizing the tools of deliberation, providing guarantees for minorities—that is, democratizing democracy.

But this political perspective excludes reflection on borders—and overlooks the thorny question of belonging. The gaze is thus concentrated on the internal—turning our backs to all that is external. It is as if borders were taken-as-read, as if a community held up by genetic descent were self-evident. So long as they are assumed to be facts of nature, such questions are expelled from the political field, or better, depoliticized. This means that politics bases itself on a non-political foundation. This is, moreover, a discriminatory foundation, one which marks a within and an outside. This coercion is exercised on the citizen, too, albeit in a different way, Though the citizen enjoys protection, she is also caught within this order, without being able to have any choice in the matter. The contemporary political order captures and banishes, includes and excludes.

This is the context in which an "immunitarian" democracy can operate. It is worth specifying, here, that this adjective is anything but harmless. Rather, it promises to harm and damage democracy. And can one truly speak of "democracy" where some are immunized but not others?

It is often forgotten that there are several different models of democracy—indeed, they sometimes stand in outright opposition. Ours is ever further from the model of the Greek *pólis*, however much we like to invoke its example. One ought not join those who indulge in a celebratory, enthusiastic vision of that model, ignoring its exclusion of women from public life and the dehumanization of slaves. Yet, for Greek citizens, involvement and participation were important.

What instead prevails in modern democracy is a model that, having first developed in the United States, has come to spread across the Western and Westernized world. It can be summarized in the formula: *noli me tangere*. This is all that the citizen requires of democracy: do not touch me. People, bodies, and ideas have to be able to exist, move, and express themselves untouched—which is to say, without being inhibited, constrained or forbidden by some external authority, at least so long as this is not utterly unavoidable. The whole tradition of liberal political thought has insisted on this negative conception of liberty. The demand is not for participation, but for protection. If the Greek citizen was interested in having a share in public power, the citizen of an immunitarian democracy first and foremost prioritizes his own security. It can be said that this is precisely the gravest limit of liberalism, which thus confuses guarantees with liberty. This negative vision undermines democracy, which is reduced to a system of immunity which has to safeguard human lives, in their multiple aspects.

As this model has imposed itself, the demands for protection have gradually increased. Alain Brossat has explained this insightfully, as he emphasizes the close connection between right and immunity. For citizens, their enjoyment of democracy often means nothing more than benefiting from rights, guarantees and defenses, in an ever more exclusive manner. *Noli me tangere* is the tacit watchword that inspires and guides that "battle for rights" in which, it is often believed, the most advanced front of civilization and progress can be identified. Of course, these struggles have been—and still are—important. Yet the real point lies elsewhere.

The condition of immunity reserved for some—the protected, the preserved, the guaranteed—is denied to others, i.e. the exposed, the rejected, the abandoned. One would wish for care, assistance, and rights for all. But this "all" is an ever more restricted sphere: it has borders, it excludes, it leaves behind remnants and leftovers. Inclusion is a much-paraded mirage; equality an empty word which now sounds like an insult. The discrepancy widens, the gap deepens. This is no longer only an apartheid against the poor. The discrimination lies precisely in the immunity, which itself digs the furrow of separation. This is true already within Western societies. And even more so outside, in the boundless hinterland of misery, in the planetary peripheries of despair and desolation. The system of guarantees and insurance policies does not reach the places where the losers of globalization live. Interned in the camps, parked in the urban voids, thrown away and piled up like refuse, they patiently await the possibility of being recycled. But the world of the disposable does not know what to do with excess. The dross brings pollution. It would be better, therefore, to keep at a distance these contaminated and contaminable remnants—the source of disease, the cause of contagion.

This other humanity—but would they then be "human"?—is inexorably delivered up to all kinds of violence. Delivered up to wars, genocides, famines, sexual exploitation, new forms of slavery, diseases. To our world's mechanisms of control and protection there corresponds, in the other world, the disorder and uninterrupted unleashing of the forces of nature. Reduced to simple bodies, these "savages" confront uncontained infections, persistent epidemics like AIDS, and deadly viruses like Ebola, which barely make the news and do not enter into the dominant narration. Deep down, the citizen signed up to liberal democracy believes that the abandonment of the rejected is a reflection of their lack of civilization.

The immunitarian paradigm is the foundation of the unperturbable frostiness displayed by the immune faced with the pain suffered by "others"— meaning, not other people in general, but those liable to contagion. Over there, well, their pain is a predictable fate, an inevitability. But over here, even the smallest onset of illness must be relieved, even the slightest trouble eliminated. This, too, is a border. Anaesthesia is part of the history of democracy. Laurent de Sutter discusses this in his book on narcocapitalism. Hence to immunize ourselves is also to anaesthetize ourselves. It allows us to watch on at even terrible injustices and the cruelest of crimes as impassive spectators, without feeling distress, without rising up in indignation. The disaster slips across the screen without leaving any trace. Though the immune citizen is connected, he is always-already unbound, exempt, beyond harm. The democratic anaesthesia takes away sensitivity and paralyses the raw nerve. To speak of "indifference," as many do, would reduce this to an individual moral choice. But in fact, it is an eminently political question. At root, even to discuss this in terms of racism would be to reduce it to just one example of the phenomenon. Rather, this is an affective tetany, a spasmodic contraction that produces an irreversible numbness.

The more exacting and exclusive the immunization of those within, the more implacable becomes the exposure of those superfluous creatures on the outside. That is how immunitarian democracy functions.

This twin-track approach is already well-illustrated by the experience of totalitarianism. Hannah Arendt's famous analysis of this phenomenon offered more than one warning in this regard. According to this reading, non-persons—the "scum of the earth" floating around between national borders—were chased back into a natural condition, into a defenseless bare life, in which it would be impossible to conserve even humanity itself. A finger was pointed in accusation against the shipwreck of human rights. Today's world believes that it has separated itself from the totalitarian past—erasing this memory with a quick dab of the sponge. But here, the twin-track has become an entrenched duality. This division is marked out by the very movement of civilization—a partition which is peddled as a struggle against barbarism and passed off as democratic progress.

Of course, the condition of immunity is no guaranteed right; rather, it is a general norm that varies even within the liberal democracies, depending on the power dynamics at play therein. If we needed evidence of this, we need only think of the bodies of women, as they risk all manner of abuse and discrimination within the workplace as well as within the walls of the home. The body of a homeless person under arrest in a police station is also anything but untouchable—or indeed, that of an elderly person relegated to a nursing home.

But the immunization that seeks to protect the body (and mind) of each citizen is an important reality. The forms of aversion multiply, the phobia toward contact spreads, and retreating into oneself becomes a spontaneous act. Indeed, it is precisely in this latter movement that we should make out the tendency of the citizen who distances himself from the *pólis* and all that he has in common with it. He no longer answers to it. He is disaffected. The immunized citizen's anaesthesia and the low intensity of his political passions make him an impassive spectator of the world's disasters. But they are also his downfall. Where immunity prevails, community declines. Roberto Esposito has explained as much, as he connects the bonds of community to the shared fear of death. Today, from time to time, a highly fleeting fear—one that is both widespread and uncertain—clots together the community of a phantasmal "us."

The Latin word *immunitas* includes the Latin root *munus*. This term is difficult to translate: it means tribute, gift, and duty, but in the sense of a debt that can never be repaid, a mutual obligation that establishes an inexorable bond. Indeed, to be exempt, to receive dispensation, is to be immune.

The opposite of the immune is the common. But individual and collective are the two mirror-image faces of the immunitarian regime. The common indicates the sharing of a mutual obligation. In no way does this mean mere fusion. To be part of a community means to be linked, bound to each other, constantly exposed, ever-vulnerable.

Hence the reason why community is constitutively open. Community cannot take the form of a self-identical fortress, closed, defended and protected. If that were so, it would instead be an immunitarian regime. Especially in recent years, a paradoxical ambiguity has developed, in which community is swapped for its opposite—immunity. This shift is plain for all to see. Thus, democracy thrashes around, caught between two opposed and irreconcilable tendencies. This is the point where its very future will be played out. Immunitarian democracy is impoverished of community—it is almost entirely bereft of it. "Community" is discussed in such a manner that it means nothing beyond a set of institutions headed by some authority principle. The citizen is subjected to those who guarantee her protection. But she is on her guard against exposure to the other, and careful to avoid the risk of contact. The other is infection, contamination, contagion.

The politics of immunization always and in every case pushes back against otherness. The border becomes the *cordon sanitaire*. All that comes from the outside reignites fear, reawakens the trauma which the citizen body believed that it had immunized itself against. The foreigner is the intruder *par excellence*. Immigration has thus come to appear as the most troubling threat.

Yet the devastating effects of immunization, including a large number of autoimmune diseases, hit citizens themselves. And perhaps only in this epochal crisis are these effects becoming clearly apparent. For example, where the sovereign administrator ends up unveiling the dark, monstrous face behind his mask—allowing people to die because of carelessness, cold-heartedness, and incompetence.

The citizen of an immunitarian democracy, precluded from sharing in the experience of the other, resigns herself to following all the rules of health and hygiene. Indeed, she has no difficulty in recognizing herself as a patient. The heterogeneous spheres of politics and medicine overlap and meld together. One cannot know where right ends and healthcare begins. Political action tends to take on a medical modality, while medical practice becomes politicized. Here, too, Nazism provided the model—however scandalous it may seem to remind ourselves of this.

The citizen-patient is more patient than citizen. For it seems that she can enjoy defenses and protections and benefit from life in that part of the world with anesthetic-immunitarian conditions. But she cannot but ask herself what the outcomes of a pastoral-medical democracy will be; she cannot but look on, worried, at the autoimmune reaction getting the upper hand.

7

GOVERNMENT BY EXPERTS:
SCIENCE AND POLITICS

Since the coronavirus gripped the public space it has set the agenda for TV news, the daily papers and commentators. But the representatives of political parties (whether in government or opposition) seem to have disappeared. The viral infection has swept the rug out from under the feet of politics. Instead, it continually repeats its intention to rely on science alone: "We should let the experts speak!"

Such statements have been greeted as if they were merely self-evident. Many commentators argue that this is the opportunity to contemplate the damage that political incompetence has wrought. In the Italian case, it seems we are passing from the conspiracy theorist "NoVax" party to the Scientific Party of the Medical State.

Every talk show that airs will pull out some expert or another. They provide a whirlwind of more or less authoritative names, a jumble of theses and hypotheses—often contradicting one another—and a tornado of figures, tables and graphics. And that's not to mention the onrush of committees of experts.

All of a sudden, experts are the masters of the public sphere. Of course, incompetence is, indeed, harmful. One can hardly just take a stab at being an economist, a jurist, or a constitutional lawyer. And still less improvise as a politician (or a philosopher!). We have paid dearly for the idea that any citizen can take on an MP's job overnight, without a care. But admitting that much does not imply swallowing a regime of expert rule. For this would pose an enormous risk to democracy. If the question of the relationship between politics and science is often—unfortunately— one that we prefer to avoid, the rise of the coronavirus has posed it in the sharpest of terms.

For politics openly to abdicate its functions to science poses serious problems. Subaltern to the diktats of the economy and reduced to an administrative governance, politics has held on to an only thin margin of autonomy—and now risks losing it entirely. For politics to abdicate, to suspend itself, would be to abandon its responsibilities. In the Medical State which appears to be rearing its head—one in which the citizen would be nothing but a patient—the experts occupy a key post.

But who are these experts? How should we understand this role, mediating between scientific knowledge and its practical consequences? The frequency with which this figure now appears ought to be related to both the hyperspecialization of science and the growing complexity that makes all decision-making into such an arduous endeavor.

Often, the term "expert" is erroneously used to mean the same thing as "scientist." But it is important to distinguish between the two. For the scientist, the results of her research are always partial and provisional. But the expert faces the pressure of public opinion, with its anxious concern not only to *know* but to *predict*. So, he needs to provide firm responses, facts to work with. Amidst the interplay of clashing political and economic interests, the expert provides a verdict credited with a scientific standing and the aura of impartiality. But we should be clear that this role is anything but neutral! And so, too, that a scientist would not see things the same way. The relationship between the expert and the scientist is marked by the friction between them.

Once the expert's verdict has been entrusted to the media—to the racing torrents of the news—it is altered, manipulated, entirely transformed. Sometimes, the expert will change his view within the course of just a few days. But in the meantime, his expertise, displayed in so many charts and numbers, has silenced and taken all responsibility away from millions of citizens.

From questions over the environment to problems of military strategy, from finance to bioethics, from space programs to epidemiology, the expert is everywhere called on to speak. His words are everywhere influential, almost like the judgement of an oracle. Yet his expertise is no guarantee. If he bears some specific knowledge, and is listened to on that basis, this does not mean that he is wiser or more experienced that others. If he knows some of the *means*, he does not necessarily have a clear view of the *ends*. Rather, he may even see them less well than others do. The expert is like Agamemnon's helmsman, who managed to bring his master to his home—where he was killed. Thus, the helmsman had to ask himself not just whether he took the right route, but whether the destination itself was right.

Faith in the lofty—even magical—virtues of the expert conceals the difficulty in choosing. And this is not only a problem of specialization. Trust is placed in those who know—or are presumed to know—precisely because this will relieve the torment of having to decide. Expert evaluation becomes a remedy for the fear of judging and choosing. This goes together with the idea that there is, indeed, a solution to be found somewhere, good and ready. Hence the enormous expectations for—and ill-placed hopes in—the expert.

The politician is glad to turn to the expert. After all, the expert ought to make her task easier by providing her with information—with the facts. In emergency situations, as in the case of coronavirus, she can even leave the whole stage up to the expert. But the risky ambivalence of this relationship immediately comes to the surface. Who is using who?

While it is, indeed, judicious to seek the expert's opinion, it is risky to give him the last word, as if his judgement were a definitive verdict, the highest court of decision-making. His unlimited authority is already standing up as sovereign in the dark sphere of the exception. Hence why a fideistic act of submission to the powers of his expertise holds unthinkable dangers in store.

Politics cannot limit itself to executing experts' indications. Then, it would be nothing more than an administration following the ideal of neutrality—and thus it would fundamentally no longer have any ideals. The "proper functioning" of things would then be a value unto itself, regardless of its content. No matter whether this is a world of justice, equality and solidarity—the important thing is that it should be well-administered. The *ends* slip into the backdrop, while the *means* of government become the decisive criterion. The politician becomes the expert in experts, the hypertechnocrat-programmer. In the best of cases, she is able to administer and choose the means of government, but she no longer knows why or to what purpose in stores—better, she is no longer able to choose which ends. Yet the torment of decision, the burden of responsibility, is the corner-stone of politics.

8

PHOBOCRACY

This could be the key word for neoliberal governance. It comes from the Greek *phóbos*, fear, and *krátos*, potent, valid, strong. It is the realm of fear, the power exercised through the systematic emergency, the protracted alarm. Fear spreads, anxiety circulates, and hatred is fomented. Confidence disappears and uncertainty prevails. The fear loses its bearings and develops into panic.

Psychopolitics is not a novelty of the present era. If fear dominates souls, then it is possible to use fear to dominate the souls of others. Machiavelli turned fear into a political category, detecting its close relationship with power. For the prince, to keep sovereignty intact by surreptitiously instilling fear is a difficult art; indeed, he must avoid this sentiment degenerating into hatred and spurring the people to revolt.

Fear pervaded all modernity, ultimately reaching the twentieth century—the century of total terror. This is often confused with tyranny, a regime which still distinguishes between friends and enemies. But totalitarian power is an iron constraint which fuses all into just one. Here, terror is not just an instrument of government but itself governs. It devours the people—that is, its own body—and already bears the seeds of its self-destruction.

And what about today? Terror has become an atmosphere. Each and every person is delivered up to the planetary void, exposed to the cosmic abyss. No direct intimidation is necessary, for the risks seem to arrive from the outside. In its seeming absence, power threatens and reassures, whips up the flame of danger and promises protection—a promise it is unable to keep. For post-totalitarian democracy demands fear and is based on fear. Hence the perverse circularity of this phobocracy.

Suspense and tension follow one after the other in a permanent condition of wakefulness, in an insomnia that brings nightmares, bedazzlement and hallucinations. Life appears to be trapped in the jaws of a constant binary between the threat of being attacked and the need to defend oneself—or better, to ward off the attack. Hence the rhythm of this life is set by the alarm—and it is a life guarded by antitheft systems, entrenched behind security doors, monitored by CCTV and surrounded by walls. Fear grows. And this is a dark fear of the other, in which a variety of worries and anxieties combine, as if by magic. The immunitarian democracies are characterised by a culture of fear. This is no spontaneous emotion. Rather, it is borne of the diffuse suggestion that there is some omnipresent danger, accustoming people to threat and a sense of extreme insecurity, up to outright terror.

Hotbeds of collective apprehension catch fire and go out again; intermittent waves of stress are induced, to the point of reaching the apex of collective hysteria. There are no strategies or clear ambitions, if not the immunitarian closing of a passive, disaggregated, depoliticized community. Thus, the phantasmal "we" temporarily submits to the emergency and to its decrees. But the grip this phobocracy exerts is ephemeral; and it risks being unseated and deposed by the sovereign virus, which now seeks to govern.

9

FULL POWERS?

Marches, processions, demonstrations, rallies—up until a few months ago, the new revolts of the twenty-first century had flowed through streets and squares around the world, from Santiago to Beirut, from Hong Kong to Barcelona, from Paris to Baghdad, and from Algiers to Buenos Aires. Feminists and antiracists, environmentalists and pacifists, the new *desobedientes*, hacktivists and NGO activists were there to protest against the sovereigntist and securitarian turn, the yawning inequalities, the destruction of the environment, the spread of debt, the discrimination and rights denied. This was no mere flare-up, with nothing to come after it.

Rather, the ungoverned had entered the stage to denounce all the limits of political governance. They occupied the city squares, that space left empty by the parties. It points back symbolically to the *agorà*, the first site of democracy and the last reserve still at the community's disposal. Being-together has meant a reaction to a world that isolates and separates. Occupation is, itself, opposition and proof of solidarity. Creative gestures, novel actions, and the frequent use of masks to expose faceless financial power, challenge a state that condemns any mask that is not its own, and to rebel against surveillance and hyperbolic identification measures. Recent times in particular have seen a challenge to the architecture of the nation, the structuring of society by citizenship, and the state-centric world order.

But what is to become of these revolts, now that the coronavirus has taken over the stage? Will this end up reinforcing police powers, the disciplining of bodies, the militarisation of public space, and repressive apparatuses? Or will conflicts explode once more? Will wrongs and injustices that have now been aggravated yet further be made a common problem, through a resurgence of struggle, casting fresh light on the invisible? In fact, new forms of dissent and unprecedented creative protests are already appearing on the balconies, on the web and on the squares—from *caceroladas* to Anonymous actions, from initiatives like the ones taken by Chile's Depresión intermedia collective to assemblies on Facebook and the #digitalstrike.

Perhaps the sovereign virus will end up destabilising state sovereignty. Of course, it must not be forgotten that healthcare, the climate, education, culture and the economy are not private possessions, and not concessions granted from above by capital, but common goods that demand a new politics around the world.

In Hungary on March 30, 2020, Viktor Orbán handed himself full powers. The official reason: to help the fight against the epidemic. No time limits were indicated, and thus the prime minister would be able to govern by decree, even abrogating laws passed by parliament, as he saw fit. The opposition decried a *coup de main*, though this did not have much echo. The European Union had been ineffective already before this viral emergency, and now it has other priorities. The exceptional measures multiply and extend their reach. A long list of governments has seized the opportunity to widen their own powers and exercise a tighter control. The *état d'urgence* in France has been renewed, and in Britain the police have been granted extraordinary powers. Trump began to define himself as a wartime president, implying that his freedom to make decisions would be extended as in times of war. Laws that suppress many individual freedoms, censor the media and allow the digital monitoring of citizens have been voted through in Bolivia, the Philippines, Thailand and Jordan. It is impossible to ignore the risk that the danger of contagion will entail a parallel epidemic of repressive and authoritarian measures.

Behind this viropolitics—or better, coronapolitics—looms the disturbing figure of the phobocratic sovereign. The reiterated declarations of war and appeals to the nation are an explicit signal of this. Among other things, they show how politics has broken down; it is unable to speak to a disaggregated community except by playing on fear and invoking the urgent need to overcome internal conflicts. The speed with which exceptional measures have been taken, along with all the juridical consequences that they imply, is explained by the precedent provided by another phantom war—the war on terror, which opened the door to the state of emergency. The warlike jargon used to narrate this unprecedented event leaves little room for doubt as to the risk of repressive moves. Yet, while the police have been deployed in the streets, there is no military mobilization.

Medicine is a battle for life; its victories are not based on death. But this does not free it of the possibility that it will be tempted to become complicit. The health crisis must not be the pretext for the opening of an authoritarian laboratory. This does not imply any hasty or naive rejection of the remedies and cures that could halt the propagation of the virus. But the securitarian and biosecuritarian measures being taken ought to be met with vigilance—and make us wary even of ourselves and our own impulses. The epidemic cannot be allowed to introduce an era of generalized suspicion in which each person appears to the other as a potential spreader, a permanent threat. The consequence would be that we would no longer have a world in common, nor even share the public space of the *pólis*.

For sure, the coronavirus is no patriot. It thumbs its nose at borders and, like it or not, globalization has gone viral. Yet the paradoxes have only accumulated. Europe issued a ban on foreigners entering even when it was itself the very hotbed and epicenter of the pandemic. This hollow, impulsive display of sovereignty was repeated with the ostentatious closing of the borders between the individual European countries. The untamed competition between them went so far as an outright refusal to send medical supplies to those in need. This lack of solidarity will surely leave an indelible trace on the memory of many of Europe's peoples. Once again, the Union proved to be a haphazard assembly of co-proprietors—a jumble of nations each defending its own particular interests, in the battle for space expressed in each shaky compromise. There is no sense of the common, here; no thought is given to community. And this is wholly to the advantage of authoritarian regimes and sovereigntist parties who have long invoked the closing of borders, national protectionism and patriotic abnegation. Was it not Matteo Salvini, leader of Italy's Lega Nord, who demanded "full powers" already long before the epidemic?

Having earlier launched a campaign of hatred against migrants, state xenophobia has found a useful new enemy in the "foreign virus." But the virus itself shows the pointlessness of the putting-up of borders and the confrontation between nation states, each confined within its territory, jealous of its own sovereignty and transfixed by the immanence of power. The sovereign virus passes through the air, and no one is immune.

10

A CONTAGION OF CONSPIRACY THEORIES

The coronavirus is an "unbelievable scam." It is the "great enemy" born in a bat's stomach. It is a test-tube apocalypse, the by-product of a chemical formula for exterminating humanity. It is a secret bacterial weapon that China has lost control of. It is a marketing strategy used by Big Pharma lobbies to increase medicine sales. It is an experiment planned and funded by Bill Gates, an enormous machination to patent the vaccine, rake in profits and gain mastery over the planet. It is a "Big Lie" orchestrated by hidden "powers that be" in order to hide the lethal effects of 5G, a technology held to have destroyed the immune system.

It is the "Wuhan virus" that broke out in the city's disturbing market in wild animals. It is the "Chinese virus" that escaped from the National Biosafety Laboratory. It was spread in Italy by US

fight for the why.

secret agents in order to block the progress of the "Silk Road" and stop the Chinese economy from penetrating into the Old Continent. It is an "American virus," a bacillus sneakily spread by five athletes who had been hospitalized in China.

In all these cases it is a "foreign virus." The mystery enveloping the virus's origins only add to the distress, exciting conspiracy-theorist fantasies and giving rise to the most outlandish interpretations and bizarre and opportunistic hypotheses. Not even political representatives have restrained themselves. Indeed, this time not just insider sources but even heads of government—first among them Donald Trump—have given vent to rumors and tall tales. The global war is also being fought through conspiracist fables.

But Bolsonaro particularly distinguished himself. He persisted to the last in playing down the virus, presenting it as just another flu, and denying that the healthcare emergency was more than a media-fueled "fantasy." This denialism found backing in the positions taken by controversial scientist Shiva Ayyadurai (who remains a doctor at MIT, Cambridge), who has repeatedly taken to Twitter to condemn "alarmism" and maintain that coronavirus "will go down in history as one of the biggest frauds to manipulate the economy, to suppress dissent, and to push mandated medicine." Conspiracy-theorist Cassandras waiting for the final catastrophe had already long previously seen a worldwide pandemic as the organized massacre that would have drastically culled humanity. It was all seen, predicted and pre-announced. And then COVID-19 came along as proof for a prophesy that had gone unheard.

Invisible by essence, the coronavirus looks like the ideal instrument in the hands of occult forces, as they secretly work away at their efforts to strip the people of their sovereignty. The anxious concern to unmask them is tinged with hatred and colored with rage.

Who will be able to resist? Who will be immune to the contagion? Fake news multiplies at an unstoppable rate. They race down the mobile flows of telecommunications devices, where they are copied, intensified and spread anew. The World Health Organization considers the infodemic— literally, the information epidemic—almost as grave a danger as COVID-19 itself. Perhaps *this* is the global virus, for which no vaccine has yet been found?

Conspiracy theories are no recent invention; they can boast of many significant forerunners in centuries past. But the twentieth century did see one unprecedented new phenomenon: the *global* spread of conspiracy-theorist myths. This has had devastating effects. We need only mention the ones concerning the Holocaust. Yet despite public censure and the widespread discredit that surrounds it, conspiracist thinking does in many regards appear to be hegemonic.

An obsessively repeated question asks, "What's going on behind the scenes?" The new culture of conspiracy theory, feeding on the unfiltered information spread online, sees plots everywhere, revealing intrigues and casting light on hidden machinations. It covers the world in enemies. There is no event—epidemics, migratory movements, terrorist attacks, wars—that does not have some guilty party behind it, its phantasmal scapegoat. At one time an extreme tool, the conspiracy theory has today become a recurrent means of propaganda. Amidst paranoia and suspicion, the conspiracist passion takes over. It builds a web of complicity ensnaring the ever more delegitimized elites—and points an accusing finger against minorities accused of seeking to manipulate the majority.

What explanation is to be found for events like the viral pandemic, whose apocalyptic charge tears such a hole in everyday existence? How can one orient oneself amidst the bracing headwinds of globalization, where war is confused with peace and the friend with the enemy? Uncertainty, dismay and fear prevail, in a world that increasingly appears as an impenetrable chaos. Perhaps, concealed behind the appearances of things, there is an occult reality that needs to be brought to light—or better, unmasked. Mysterious forces and "the hidden powers that-be" are controlling the planet's fate.

Conspiracists' fables are easy to propagate and hard to refute. They respond to demands that are now being subjected to a difficult test—the need to explain and to believe. The farewell bid to traditional religions and political ideologies has opened the way for all manner of gullible credulity and obstinate dogmatism. Absent any obvious causes, it is better to have faith in whatever responds to one's own convictions, and fits with one's own expectations. No matter the evidence and proofs showing the opposite is true. The decisive question is what argument is most *useful*: the practical effect strengthens the myth, which can thus withstand all criticism. A disease that afflicts a disenchanted world, the conspiracy-theorist fantasy satisfies the demand for certainty, the need for transparency, the boundless desire to explain and rationalise everything. Faced with complexity, better to choose the shortcut of simplification. Thus re-emerges the dream of finding a sense to things at all costs—and all the more so if the landscape is hard to read.

To believe in conspiracy is to accept a summary, magical conception of history in which everything can be traced back to a single cause, acting intentionally through a persistent subjective will. The more intricate the scenario seems, the greater the mania to find some ultimate explanation. Hence the analogy with mythical thinking. The effectiveness of a myth does not lie in its truthfulness, but rather in the demands to which it responds, the emotions it stirs and its suggestive power. So, it would be misleading to speak of "falsehood" and truths being denied. For a myth does not deny anything: it stops at telling its own story. This is the great power of fiction. This is why it is pointless to show that tall tales are groundless: and that master of conspiracy, Hitler, was glad to recognize as much.

Wielding his imaginary political science, the conspiracy theorist does not just intend to decipher the course of events; he also claims to oversee it, to give it direction. Convinced that he holds the key to history, which will allow him to resolve all problems and eliminate all sources of anxiety, he operates in a Manichean perspective in which Evil stems from a concealed, arcane world-behind that must finally be brought out into the open. His job is to flush out the enemy and uncover the threat. Yet this act of occult magic is also a symbolic act of war. The conspiracy theorist does not stop at his flight into chimeras and illusions; when he identifies the dark forces into whose hands the world has fallen, he does so with the intention of opposing them. He claims a victim role for himself and constructs an absolute enemy, in each instance defined by its supposed objectives: decimation, spoliation, domination. The more metaphysically abstract this enemy—like "the elites," "the caste," the "world government"—the more fearsome and detested it is. It should not be forgotten how key conspiracy theories are to a certain populism.

Today, all this is aggravated by the volatility of power. This is not because power has gone away—quite the opposite! But it is distant, fleeting, ubiquitous, projected along the paths of technology and the flows of the economy, lacking any center and perhaps any direction. It has no name, no face, no address. The malaise reported by those struck by power lies precisely in the fact that it is so difficult to locate it. All that can be perceived is its diffuse presence. If there is an effect, then there must also be a cause. Skepticism turns into a dogmatic certainty that there must be some hidden center of power. Hence why the gloomy phantasms of conspiracy that infest the political landscape are today multiplying.

But one cannot overlook the fact that what encourages this dismal disposition is the culture of fear. Conspiracy theory is the other side of the coin to phobocracy. An impoverished, hypocritical politics whose ability to govern relies on it continually off-loading its own responsibilities onto whatever enemy is at hand—the immigrant, the "gypsy," Brussels bureaucrats, the "Chinese virus"—is the inexhaustible source of conspiracy-theorist fantasies. It is no accident that the number of governments that make recourse to such tools is rising, even when it comes to their international relations.

It isn't much use demonizing conspiracy-theorizing: ultimately, it is itself a symptom. And not necessarily a negative one: it expresses the desire, however naive, to understand more and get a clear view of things. To assume that it is a disease that only afflicts a handful of paranoid madmen would itself be a conspiracist approach, blaming the world's ills on some shady clique plotting in the conspirosphere. As Rob Brotherton has observed, we are all a little conspiracy theorist—so better to admit it than just let ourselves off the hook.

The conspiracy theory is not a viral disease that needs defeating and rooting out. The war on conspiracism is just as absurd as the war on the virus. The important thing is to find means of coexistence, not to seek to immunize ourselves. Sometimes, a contagious paranoia can even be useful caution. So long as the medicine is in the right doses.

11

KEEPING A DISTANCE

)
breaking of
community

Thermal scanning systems in airports, territorial controls, quarantines for the potentially infected, and then masks, precautionary measures and frequent hand washing. Will all this be enough?

The prospect of contact stirs up stress, and the fear of contamination becomes palpable as it insinuates itself into everyday life. Better to avoid public places and lock ourselves away in the private domestic space. This niche, scattered with screens with which we can look out at the world, protected, has never seemed so indispensable.

Distance does not everywhere mean the same thing: for the distribution of bodies across the public space has different labels, rituals and habits. Even among European countries, distance gets narrower as one moves, for example, from Finnish to German and then Italian cities, where almost every encounter is imbued with effusive kissing and hugging. Norbert Elias has written about the norms underlying these processes, which are ever less neutral and ever more neurotic.

Stories of the plague tell of the *effect* of contagion, in driving each person to isolate themselves as much as possible. They feared the other, identifying them as a potential spreader, and thus came to consider distance itself as the only hope, the sole effective remedy. Yet in immunitarian democracies—which are thus impossible to immediately compare with the past—the fear of being touched, which always characterizes distancing, is already a *phobia* of contagion. "There is nothing that man fears more than the touch of the unknown"—this famous statement by Elias Canetti does not stand in abstraction from any context, but refers to our modern habitations. We close ourselves off in our homes, where no one can enter—and where we feel relatively secure.

The right to the integrity of the domestic sphere provided the foundations on which old-European law was built. But now, the habitation makes it possible to delimit an area of protection and well-being, against possible invaders and those with malign intentions. May the community be banished! What counts is one's right to defend oneself against disturbances coming from the outside—without having to justify oneself. Habitation is a sort of extension of the body, allowing for a peculiar self-representation and a likewise special self-care. Both have become habits. Habitation expresses the need for a reassuring closedness and brings to light the emergence of the immunitarian paradigm. Human openness toward the world is ever more precluded by the powerful impulse to avoid it. Hence also the widespread spatial resentment—the sovereigntist jealousy for the place one inhabits. We need only think of the much-touted myths of "invasion" and the diffuse fear of the immigrant.

The legal imposition of distance is a preventative policing of relations—a regulatory shield that protects us from family members as from those unknown to us. This is only the climax of a political process that had been underway already beforehand. The other is now abolished *by decree*, in exchange for security and immunity. Indeed, the body of the individual citizen is a fortress that must be safeguarded against countless dangers and unthinkable threats. Relations are now distinguished by circumspection and suspicion—and they are also necessarily mediated by devices capable of separating, containing, making-secure and preserving. Hence "social distancing" applies the seal of immunitarian politics.

In a certain sense, it can be said—with dismay—that when all physical contact is banned by law, as a source of contagion, a risk of tarnishment and contamination, the cycle of civilisation comes to an end.

The open, spontaneous, hospitable community—of assembly, of play, of dance, of celebration—thus seems to disappear from the civic and political horizon. The community outside the state and outside the institutions, the community of the ecstatic movement of the self that extends toward the other, exposes itself, abandons itself, falls under the blows dealt by the decrees. What remains is hyper-protected, regimented, screened-off—the shadow of community.

The disturbing aspect of the measures taken, faced with the COVID-19 emergency, is not only the fact of being distanced from the other and the implicit veto it sets up against any embrace, any spontaneous effusiveness. Also disturbing is the darkness cast by the ban on all unprotected relations—the relations of co-presence and encounter among bodies. The consequences are political.

This is the sense in which one ought to detect, here, the laboratory of new and unprecedented types of order.

The citizen-patient, for whom the experience of the other is now precluded, resigns herself to the regulation of distance, submits to the sanitary norms that extend their grip over the sexual and affective sphere. Sometimes she is overwhelmed by a gloomy nostalgia for the crowd, in which she would like to once again immerse herself and thus exorcise the phobia of contact. Canetti shed light on this in his famous masterpiece *Crowds and Power*:

> It is only in a crowd that man can become free of this fear of being touched. That is the only situation in which the fear changes into its opposite. The crowd he needs is the dense crowd, in which body is pressed to body; a crowd, too, whose psychical constitution is also dense, or compact, so that he no longer notices who it is that presses against him. As soon as a man has surrendered himself to the crowd, he ceases to fear its touch. ... The more fiercely people press together, the more certain they feel that they do not fear each other. This reversal of the fear of being touched belongs to the nature of crowds.

Avoiding the crowd, banning it by law, does not mean encouraging individualism. The question is quite a different one. For some time, the phobia of the crowd has accompanied massified society. This is no paradox. For they are but two sides of the same coin. But becoming-crowd in the public space had already been disciplined, or accepted only in a closely calculable and calculated way: in official celebrations or at sports grounds or concerts. This crowd, unlike the one described by Canetti, is itself rarefied, based on a prohibition of others, pre-arranged, filtered and surveilled.

One cannot help but think that what is at work here is an attempt to ward off conflict, by providing a simulacrum of civil war, especially through certain forms of competition like football. Yet the immunisation dictated by COVID-19 arrives at the most extreme proportions. And among other things, it has struck in a period marked by global revolts. It is not, then, ever so difficult to read the warning that immunitarian democracy issues: it removes the danger of the living, uncontrollable crowd and puts the spectre of revolt at a distance, by ensuring the sanitary conditions for survival.

It is well-known that the fabric of distance is woven with strands of closeness—and vice versa. But the apparently sterile term "distancing" means something very different. The mass is separated from the weight of bodies, pruned of physical resistance, placed at the disposal of an uninterrupted, non-stop flow of messages, 24 hours a day. Relations are put behind screens, through the media interposed in between.

But, again in this context, one should not ignore the continuity that is going on alongside the obvious change. For years now, our peers have been increasingly placed at a distance—a process realized through the ever more powerful develop-ment of media platforms and the expansion of communicative ideology. The public square and spontaneous sites of encounter have been increasingly supplanted by the virtual space of the web. The face-to-face encounter based on physical proximity to the other—a source of apprehension, a reserve of surprises, a haven of unexpected calm—has given way to a situation in which our senses are denied contact with our peers.

"Social distancing" confines the—infected, infectious, infectable—body and consigns it to an aseptic, sterile virtuality. This is a defeat for those who hold that the body is a breach in techno-libertarian hegemony. The body is rather more perceived as lack, as a privation. Others' bodies no less than one's own. Contact itself is contaminated by contagion.

To live and work "remotely" is to be surrounded by screens. The ambiguity of the screen encapsulates the entire immunitarian paradigm. As the screen protects, shelters and shields, it also opens up access to the world. No one considers screens mere surfaces—even if one accepts that this was ever the case in the past. And without doubt, during this period of distancing their uses have multiplied and diversified, from videoconferences to the meals "eaten together." But how far is it possible to speak of "screen experiences," as some propose? The relationship with the screen is not the same as the relationship with the gaze. Digital exploration does not have the sensitivity or still less the tactile quality of the organic senses. The eye can draw infinitely close to the surface and still be light years away from it, separated by a space that the body can never cross.

The digital medium interposes itself, separating even as it allows communication. Whatever it brings together, it also puts at a distance. This is, at root, precisely the reason why this means of communication is celebrated and fetishized. Its mediation allows one to ensure the other's availability, without ever being weighed down by presence. These are also the convenient and advantageous aspects of "distance learning," which some have gone so far as to praise.

Distancing is the code of communication in the immunitarian age. The McWorld, the enormous online space in which each person has now acquired a further citizenship, is studded with impersonal virtual communities. These forced proximities—these temporary, chance synergies—flow from chats, blogs, and social networks. They are the meeting points of our centrifugal paths through the web, which often come to an abrupt halt—leaving nothing but the void. Hence the dependency, the breathless effort to stay connected. Indeed, there is no guarantee of not ending up excluded, abandoned, in the waste bin of technology. The "us" of the political community cannot be constituted from the landscape built on the web.

12

A MENTAL HEALTH PANDEMIC

Fevers, dry coughs—and above all, anxiety. The line outside the pharmacy is stretching ever longer. The discontent and impatience are growing. It seems that the few masks that did arrive are already running short. One person is chatting away on the phone; another steps back to peek inside, nervously. Whenever another person moves it is grounds for suspicion; anyone not paying attention is cause for apprehension. The next in line is contagious—and contagion is next in line. The solitude of the metropolis is encapsulated in this gloomy queue; here and there, the old shadows of competition pop up. There is no hint of affability or courtesy. Rather, this is the time of aggressive mediocrity. Whoever has managed to lay their hands on the sought-after commodity hurries away, both nervous and oblivious, withdrawn into themselves.

If the initial panic was exorcised on the balconies, it has been replaced by a sense of ruefulness, of stunned, bitter resignation. How long will it be? When will all this stop? Those who were convinced this was just a normal flu have to think again, however unwillingly. Aversion, frustration and unease beat the rhythm of everyday life.

If the coronavirus strikes at the body, the pandemic is also a mental health emergency. This is little discussed in public debate—it's almost as if this were a taboo, something to cast a veil over. But who decides what is vitally important? Each person is compelled to acknowledge their fragility and their mortality. They have to stay alive, protect themselves, defend their living organism. But the restrictions designed to save lives also have harmful effects on existence itself, paralyzing human relations and blocking off affective contacts. In some cases, the lack of others may even be deadly. The tragedy of suicide is very much today's reality.

The mass house arrests risk a mental health implosion of the most unthinkable consequences. One fear comes after another: the fear of falling ill, of losing one's job, of being abandoned, of ending up attached to a ventilator. The viral shock produces sadness, rage, irritability, depression, insomnia. It can hardly be assumed that the only ones to be hit hard by confinement will be those who already had mental health problems. Many people's existence has transformed overnight—it seems that it is being swallowed up by the void. Their work, the activities of a lifetime, their frenetic routine, are all suddenly suspended. Friends, relatives and acquaintances are now only distant voices, faces filtered by screens. Technology makes the distance much less unbearable, while there is an ever-clearer difference between forced isolation and the solitude one seeks and yearns for.

This is an existence between parentheses—one tolerated with great difficulty, in the spasmodic expectation that the waiting will ultimately end. As the malaise becomes more protracted, it also sharpens. This is all the more true as the idea gains traction that the forms of our life will never be the same again—that life will be changed even in the slightest details, and perhaps reorganized at a global level.

Not everyone has the means to cope with this anxious existence between parentheses—or the capacity to work through their distress. The vain, self-satisfied vogue for diaries is echoed by the heaps of consultants and influencers, the latest pseudo-thinkers who regale us with cut-price solutions and advice which no one asked for.

As for those restless lives who stand waiting at the window of quarantine—those not hooked on the drug of stress—they simply get bored. The duration of time is excruciating; its extent is all blurred; its stretch is only internal, as everything appears indifferent and devoid of meaning. The bustle of life, its many different pushes and pulls, is replaced with an unyielding boredom in which there is nothing to do but kill time. The virus thus brings out into the open what philosophers have called inauthenticity—the absence of a life-project. We suffer the fear of being deprived of the world, and the tedium of detachment from our own dispersed, much-occupied selves. The boredom is not the threshold to a reawakening, a new light cast on existence. Walter Benjamin's words come to mind, here: "Boredom is the dream bird that hatches the egg of experience. A rustling in the leaves drives him away. His nesting places—the activities that are intimately associated with boredom—are already extinct in the cities and are declining in the country as well."

13

CONFINEMENT AND DIGITAL SURVEILLANCE

Locked down in my room, my gaze passing back and forth between the walls, my thoughts suddenly turned to the experience of those whose everyday life is reclusion—those who share their limited space with others, and suffer time inflicted in all its naked force. Prison is the always-the-same without a future; it is incarcerated time.

If we are anaesthetized from others' miseries, this is all the truer if they have been locked up. We look at them through the state's eyes. The penitentiary desolation must not filter out. Being invisible and abandoned is part of the sentence. "Lock 'em up and throw away the key!" These ever more frequently uttered words are colored by a smugly vindictive cold-heartedness. The securitarian brutalization wants more walls, more barbed wire, more prisons. Some moderates ask for less overcrowding and more "legality."

The whole problem is reduced to that. Is legality in prison not a contradiction in terms? To be walled in, amidst promiscuity, lack of care, and the breaking of all relations, is supposed to have a restorative, corrective function. If that were not true (and there's plenty reason for doubt) it would then be necessary to admit that the cities are studded with factories processing a sub-humanity expelled from the common world, banished from citizenship. In large part that means poor people, the unemployed, immigrants, nomads, prostitutes, pot smokers.

When the first anti-contagion measures were imposed in Italy, revolts broke out in the jails—in Rome, Venice, Rimini, and Naples. A few images from the revolts did make it to our screens: anti-riot cops, flying squads, drones, tear gas. They told us that thirteen, maybe fifteen, prisoners were dead, killed by the methadone they found in the jails' medicine cabinets. The bodies did not have any wounds on them. Then the whole matter was forgotten. Not to leave a trace—that's the reason they were in prison to begin with.

On April 2, 2020, almost four billion people—around half of the world's inhabitants—had received government orders or appeals to stay at home. The measures to contain the spread of COVID-19 were isolation, quarantine, and in some cases, curfew. The Italian government decree, retweeted everywhere, proclaimed: #iorestoacasa—I'm staying at home. It is an episode without precedent.

Confinement is a tacit new frontier established within our private existence. This is going to be for a few months? Well, there's no choice but to resign ourselves to it. Or, will it become an effective general security measure—one that applies even after the epidemic? Mass house arrests are a singular suspension of time in which everything is slowed down. Time is arrested, as if as a metaphor for a historical era pitched into reiteration. Factories, offices, schools, universities, shops, malls, bars, restaurants, cinemas, theaters, stadiums, even churches, synagogues and mosques—all closed. Each person stands alone before an enormous void. Community seems lost. The applause and the singing on the balconies, the countless live broadcasts on Instagram and Facebook, are nothing but vain efforts to reproduce community, improvised rituals for processing grief. We lament the *pólis* that has now disappeared. The public space has retreated; at most, there remains a mere semblance of it.

Will this contribute to a further depoliticisation of life?

Putting half the world under house arrest does not imply a generalized imprisonment. Any such comparison would be senseless. However severe the restrictive measures, and however great the threat from the panopticisation of a video-surveilled, monitored, patrolled society, the threshold represented by the jailhouse has not disappeared. On the one side is the imprisoned world, and on the other, the world outside. The difference is still there.

Some of the infected die; but those who have been confined, put at a distance, abandoned, can die too... So perhaps it would be better to accept digital assistance, temporarily at least? Contact tracing, apps giving proof of immunity, apps for self-diagnosis, thermal lenses and oximeters, radar to detect the COVID-positive, platforms for epidemiological data and diagnostic tests. We will be traced, monitored, GPS-located. This is partly the case already. So, why not profit from the digital wind blowing through the immaterial cables? Why not unleash it, in the race against the coronavirus? Digital communication is viral? Perhaps we could get the jump on COVID-19 and defeat it on its own terrain—or better, in the airflow.

There, in all its ambivalence, is the choice between confinement and digital control. Different cultures push in different directions. In Asian countries, the collection of personal data is now an acquired habit, as is a full record-keeping on citizens—and sometimes, this even means rating them. All this would be unthinkable in European countries. Especially on these themes, there is a very developed critical sense. Yet faced with the brutal scenario that is confinement—an extreme version of distancing—it becomes difficult to resist.

As in other spheres, the virus has a capacity to illuminate, and sheds light on our complicated relationship with digital devices. On the one hand, we cannot do without them—for this would mean being deprived of virtual contacts, no longer being informed, and leaving McWorld behind. On the other hand, we would not want these devices to become a constant source of information that allows us to be followed everywhere—spied upon in our private lives, with even our bodily functions watched and judged. There have, indeed, been cases that have sparked uproar and driven reflection. In South Korea, where the contagion is digitally traced, the movements of infected citizens have been broadcast, thus exposing them to public humiliation. In China, they have even rolled out an app that checking a person's health status, gives them a red, green or yellow code that allows them to leave their own home, go to work, or walk into a shop or restaurant.

Once what was initially traumatic has turned into a habit, it risks going unnoticed. Even if these digital processes may be necessary measures today, what certainty is there that they will go away once the emergency is over? How far will governments benefit from this—not to mention big business?

The enthusiasm for transparency is easy to agree with, in an era in which mutual trust is subject to the difficult test of distance, and a generalized traceability seems to compensate for the proximity that has been lost. But transparency establishes a regime of permanent visibility, where all are handed over to a potential inquisition. Who knows what word, what gesture, what move could one day provide the lead for an indictment which, though still indefinite, is already hanging over us. Is the coronavirus thrusting us ahead into the era of digital psychopolitics?

The surveillance online, on that gigantic web where each person is spied upon by an immense invisible eye behind the screen, is the ultimate version of the panopticon. It's just that people accept being banished into a world of total transparency—indeed, readily so.

14

RUTHLESS GROWTH

On March 8, Italy was not yet a "red zone"—but there was an exponential rise in the numbers being hospitalized with COVID-19. That afternoon I received a disconsolate WhatsApp message from a cardiologist, working in an intensive care ward in a Milan hospital. She gave a detailed description of the tragic situation—and dwelt, in the starkest of tones, on the terrible job of having to choose who had "most hope of survival."

The ventilators were not enough—or not for everyone. Those of the most advanced years, and those who already had other illnesses, were discarded as they arrived at the ward, in accordance with the criteria of "clinical ethics." This happened elsewhere in Europe, too—and all the more so in the United States. At first, public opinion seemed reluctant to believe it; then, the incredulity turned into deep indignation.

The disastrous effects neoliberalism has had on public healthcare were becoming apparent.

But there was a further symbolic shock, which added to the intensity of the first, and further wounded the sense of omnipotence. Negligence regarding the risk of infection, a lack of preventative measures, and an ill-placed confidence in their capacity to look after the sick even in an emergency situation, led many Western countries' healthcare systems to paralysis. This was symptomatic of a politics that believes itself shielded from unforeseen events by the existence of an interconnected market and its enlightened control-rooms. Thus, private profit prevailed over the public good of healthcare; the interests of pharmaceutical firms, corporate power and the producers' business concerns had the priority over citizens' lives.

The lack of the medical supplies and personnel that a prompt reaction demanded; the airing of "herd immunity" as the basis for a response; and the sys-tematic denial of the pandemic are but different aspects of capitalism's ruthlessness. They are obviously not immediately comparable, but that takes nothing away from this observation: indeed, capitalism here displayed its most devious and repugnant side. Yet, it is possible that so long as the pandemic threat remains impressed upon the common consciousness, a health crisis like this will also provide an opportunity to reengage the struggle not only for public health, but also for the preservation of the environment and of biodiversity. Zoonotic diseases—those transmitted from animals to humans—are not the result of a curse or a natural disaster, but the mark of an ecosystem that has already been all but destroyed.

The coronavirus pandemic has often been compared to other events that have shaken human history in the past. These even include ones like the Lisbon earthquake of 1755; rather more frequently mentioned are the Black Death of 1348 and the Spanish flu of 1918 to 1920, which each killed millions of people. While we should not overlook the possible similarities with such events, it is worth emphasizing that the current pandemic, which broke out in a globalized world, is truly without precedent, even simply because of the enormous speed with which the contagion spread. Its speed owes not only to the aggressive character of the virus itself, but also to the accelerated flows of traffic circulating around the world. Thus, even the reach of this pandemic has proven distinctive: today, no geographical area is spared.

Also decisive is the symbolic value of this shock, with its inevitable implications for an economic crisis which is itself unprecedented. The International Monetary Fund has said, "We've never seen the world economy standing still." It is not difficult to predict what lies ahead: recession, ruin for many people, irreversible destitution for the already poor, hunger and shortages in African countries. Thousands and thousands of migrants will again tempt fate, in their bid to cross the sea and make it to the ports of Europe.

However strange it may sound, the Black Death of 1348 presents a good point of reference to reflect upon. Why go so far back in time? That terrible epidemic also marked a historic watershed. What shines through from the extant accounts and chronicles is the survivors' sensation of having entered into a different era. The sky had closed over the other era, which had now passed. Those spared the nauseating, cruel death of this apocalypse—one that had reaped millions of victims, one third of the European population— now grasped life with an uncommon enthusiasm, a feverish ardor.

To that first epidemic in the cities was born the civic world of the Renaissance. But the new beginning also gave way to the contagion of enrichment. Affluence and monetary advantage assumed an importance they had not had before. For many this was a farewell not only to the peasant lifestyle and to the agricultural world that had so exposed them to the elements, but also to natural growth, the wait for the coming and going of the seasons, and the simple cycle of reproduction. Patience and resignation gave way to boldness and derring-do. Genoese navigators and Venetian merchants began the era of European expansion and entrepreneurial modernity, an age which set off across the ocean in search of the possible, the impossible, and most importantly, the profitable. Here came the first banks and the accumulation of capital. And like this fatal leap into the sea, the immediate revenue— the superprofits magically increased three-fold or ten-fold—would transform life itself, turning it into a dream.

The great European—and then Western— dream of globalization would last for centuries, until the nightmares started piling up. Profit proved to be not only the marker of injustice, the guarantee of the poverty of the many, but also an asphyxiating blind alley. In a bizarre paradox (which has already been noted) today "growth" is taken to mean not care for the world, but rather profit and superprofits. So it should be no surprise that the term "growth" has now taken on negative connotations, and refers less to GDP numbers than to everything we ought to avoid: the growth in illicit earnings, in waste and refuse, in illness and intoxication, in abuse and discrimination. This does not imply favoring or promoting degrowth. Perhaps it is high time that we abandoned the language of calculation and balance-sheets, dropping a banner of "growth" which no one seems to believe in anymore. It is capital that produces misery. In a landscape in which other forms of wealth have lost their meaning, what stands out on the horizon is a future of convivial sobriety, shorn of the superfluous. Such a future would bring to light the otherwise forgotten bonds of existence.

A warning and portent harbored in Europe's memory, the Black Death ought to teach us that it is always still possible to rearticulate the forms of life. It ought to teach us the need to ask ourselves what we will live for in the future. And teach us that it is indispensable that we look out toward the final frontiers that we have forgotten to dream about.

15

ISOLATING THE VICTIMS

On the night of March 18, 2020, a flight attendant watching from her balcony filmed a long column of military trucks leaving the Bergamo cemetery, as they took the coffins of the dead to other cities. The crematorium oven was no longer able to work through the excess number of corpses. The trucks' headlamps flashed almost as if apologetically, as if bemoaning their task—a duty that they would never have imagined having to shoulder. The video soon began doing the rounds online, producing deep trauma around Italy. These images seemed almost to have burst out of the darkness of the wartime past, a wound that had never healed. And they were images of a right that had here gone denied—the collective ritual of saying goodbye.

A few days later, the New York Times *published a few of the photos taken by Fabio Bucciarelli—the full* set appeared in L'Espresso. These were fragments of a night in provincial Lombardy. But all who had lived this same drama, from China to Spain, could recognize themselves in this anguished and moving kaleidoscope, in a succession of lost gazes, moments of convulsion and ghostly scenes.

How does one die of COVID-19? For the most elderly, the ambulance sirens evoke those other sirens from back in the days of World War II—the sign that the bombers were coming. The volunteers and nurses are wearing special overalls and masks. Their appearance is disturbing. Humanity shines through from their gestures and from the still-uncovered folds of their faces. They come to separate children from parents. A whole generation, the guardian of memory, is being taken away. Neighbors look on, broken, and wary. The virus offers no pardon. It all begins with a generic sense of feeling ill and a dry cough that could be taken for a symptom of any other flu. But not this time. The virus deceives and misleads. The shortness of breath intensifies, each gasp becomes quicker and shallower. The bluish lips indicate hypoxemia—the lack of oxygen. This good had been forgotten, hidden by so many other consumer goods for which there is no such need.

Everyday life is captured in the photos, in the long moments of separation. The surrounding objects—a *mirror, a lamp, a shelf crowded with mementos—no longer seem to have any meaning. There are those who refuse to leave—better to die at home. Others allow themselves to be taken away for this decisive battle. The relatives stay behind; the virus keeps them at a distance. And they are riven by guilty feelings: by sending a mother away like this to die alone. The ambulance races toward a hospital already packed with ill people. Those who get admitted are the lucky ones. In the intensive care units, places are reserved for those coronavirus patients who have a "reasonable chance of survival." The oldest are not put on ventilators; they are left to fend for themselves. In some cases, the demise is discovered only afterwards. They died alone. And this is a different solitude to the one that always accompanies a person's final moments. For the virus has already isolated them in advance. The patient struggles for breath tubed-up, attached to a machine, their head inside a transparent plastic container, without friends or relatives at their side. Not even a gesture of acknowledgement, the final salute, the simulacrum of a farewell. On a tablet screen, a strained shadow slips away. This solitude is icy, suffocating. Doctors and nurses come around, concerned, attentive, tireless. And they are all the same, covered, screened, protected. Angels of life, angels of death, who then have to surrender.*

The morgues in the hospitals no longer have enough room for all the corpses. The religious rites are reduced to a few gestures, prayers barely murmured. Funerals are banned. Even the cemetery itself is sealed off. Bodies cannot be given the sorrowful ritual treatments dating to time immemorial. They have to be cremated with what they were wearing at the moment of their demise, sheathed in a disinfecting fabric. The bureaucracy speeds up and the death certificate quickly arrives. The coffins are loaded five or six at a time. With no one to accompany them. There are not even flowers, for the florists have been closed. The army trucks set off again. Their funereal procession extends along the motorways, the junctions, the ring roads, escorted by police patrols. The dead must not disturb the city of the living. But under these camouflaged tarps, ever the same, are the tobacconist, the retired schoolteacher, the pastor to the poor, the warden, the pharmacist, the lady from the third floor, an elderly married couple who died together. Provincial stories both big and small, suddenly extinguished by a History that has taken on an apocalyptic rhythm in recent times. So, it all ends. The relatives are given the ashes. But it's rather more of a hazard to deliver the plastic bag with the dead person's personal effects: a pair of slippers, a tin of biscuits, a watch.

Death has always, more or less tacitly, been considered contagious. The living draw away from it. For evidence of this we need only look at the countless accounts of the plague, that scourge on centuries past. Thucydides spoke of it already in his day. But today death represents such a danger to life that it has definitively disappeared behind the wings of the public stage. This is not so much an existential suppression of death, as its political negation.

In today's sanitizing culture, death has to be cleaned up, disinfected, sterilized—to the point that it is exorcized and denied. It's the same thing that happens to radioactive waste and bacterial residues. That death is now being produced by an unknown virus makes all this clearly plain to see, driving it toward a remarkable hyperbole. The threat that now looms is another hurried lockdown—one to isolate the victims themselves.

The communal graves, discovered here and there by drones, provide a telling proof of this. The troubling, repugnant thing, here, is not only the means of burial, even when it is so fiercely sterile and so mercilessly perfunctory. Also troubling is the purging of death from the city. This happened in New York, where the bodies of those without names, families or money were offloaded on Hart Island, the gloomy rock to the east of the Bronx.

As the contagion advanced, the dead in the mortuaries could no longer be counted, and the cemeteries filled up. So, it was necessary to hasten to get rid of the bodies of those who could never have afforded a funeral—the bodies of the poor already destined to die badly. This was already custom and practice on this "island of the dead"—but the pandemic shed light on it.

There is a similar situation among the elderly people who have literally disappeared from rest homes, all over the world. No one knows how many dead there are, but their numbers are myriad. It will never be possible to produce an accurate list of them. But behind these numbers, the charts and tables, is a whole generation is being wiped out. They have disappeared just like that—often left to die without treatment, cut down by the virus. And this virus has been able to operate with ease in closed places like institutes, convents and prisons.

In some places, they are given the rather less harsh label of "rest homes"—a name sometimes further softened with some acronym. But they are the great parking lot assigned to the Third Age. The fight to make life longer goes on, but we no longer know what to do with old age and the elderly, now stripped of the prestige of times past, and reduced to dead weight. The "rest home" has nothing relaxing about it; it is, rather, an empty space where old age is segregated and swept away, before death. Old age is subjected to the same discrimination as death itself.

In the past, death would enter back into the public space. Up until a few decades ago, in the cities of Southern Italy the funeral carriage would pass along the main avenue, amidst the closed shutters of the shops and the simultaneous gestures of those taking off their hats as a sign of respect faced with the majesty of death. Now, distancing has reached its apogee, becoming an outright separation. The dying person dies anonymously in the clinics where they had already been confined beforehand. And death is inserted within the cycle of economic production. Through technological devices and sedative drugs, the experience of death is taken away from those who die—but at root, also from those who survive. The eclipse of death has now been institutionalized.

Public life does not want to be disturbed by this incurable deviance, this unthinkable anomaly. Heidegger issued a warning against the recurrent, everyday mode of erasing death—meaning, that which shoos it away from thought and follows along with the chatter which makes it appear as a constant "not-yet." Death happens, but no one dies. It is something that happens to other people, not to me. This is the misunderstanding suggested by the spectacularization of death, turning it into a mere semblance of itself.

But this erasure is intensifying and consolidating, in the complete separation which reaches its endpoint in advanced capitalism. The dead cease to exist. They are proscribed, pushed back, put at the greatest possible distance from the city center, in a fixed-term burial ground or an urn. Cremation is the peak of this subtle liquidation, this complete deconsecration. A deathly silence prevails. No longer is it to be discussed. Life must be purged of death. The wellbeing of others, the living, can no longer be tarnished and corrupted by something so obscene, distasteful, unpresentable as death. The common feeling that was once expressed in the rituals for the deceased, in the articulation of grief, falls into disuse, its flame extinguished.

The attempt to put an end to death—to erase it, to vanish it away—is a characteristic trait of capitalism, of its compulsion for growth, of its logic of accumulation. As Byung-Chul Han explained in a recent essay, "Capitalism's compulsive accumulation and growth is specifically aimed against death, which counts as absolute loss." It is imagined that this is a way of growing our capacity to survive, of immunizing ourselves against death. More capital and less death—in an epic conflict, a final confrontation dictated by the transhuman dream of immortality.

But in its obsessive quest for an a-mortal life, capitalism ends up achieving the very opposite. If the factory no longer exists, labor is ubiquitous; and if death is disappeared away and bodies are treated as infectious waste, the city itself becomes a necropolis—an ascetic, sterile space of death.

History ought to teach something else: that the offense done to the dignity of death undermines the entire community, prevents the labor of mourning, and inhibits memory. The impossibility of working through the past suspends the present and sets up barriers to the future. This is what makes the individual gestures bidding farewell and the collective rituals of loss so indispensable. Death is irreversible, but this does not reduce it to negativity alone. For non-believers, too, redeeming others' death is a duty. Those who survive are summoned to respond—they have a responsibility that goes beyond the sense of guilt that torments them, beyond the obligation to show deference. When the other dies, what also comes to the end is her unique, irreplaceable world—which was also a little bit mine, and ours. Here comes the loss of a world, a loss of memory. If we are to avoid a spectral grief, an ineluctable bewilderment, then distancing must not have the summary result of locking down the victims.

16

BREATHING MEETS WITH CATASTROPHE:
ARE WE IN THE CLEAR?

*Perhaps we will come out of this with immunity cer-
tificates to vouch for our antibodies. We will pass
through sophisticated thermoscanners and dense cir-
cuits of video surveillance, almost as if by habit, in
sanitized places and non-places. We will maintain the
security distance and warily look about, distrustful of
what surrounds us. The masks will not be much help
in distinguishing our friends and being recognized by
them. We will long continue to detect asymptomatic
cases all around us, unknowingly harboring the
intangible threat of contagion. Perhaps the virus will
already have been removed from the air, dissolved and
disappeared away, but its ghost will long remain. And
we will still be gasping, short of breath.*

*We will be able to retell the epoch-defining event
we have lived through. And we will do so as survivors—though perhaps we will be unaware of the*

risks that this conceals. These risks do not only owe to the insidious effects of suppressing this past. Nor do they only owe that the commitment incumbent on life, to redeem and repay the life that is no more, in the infinite labor of grief. Survival can be inebriating and elating; it can become a sort of pleasure, an insatiable satisfaction, that some may even take for a triumph. Those who have lived beyond—thus escaping the fate that crashed down on others' heads—feel favored and privileged. As Canetti observed, this sensation of strength may even win out over the distress. It is as if the survivors had given a good show of themselves and were somehow better. With the danger now banished, they have an extraordinary, exciting impression of invulnerability. But this powerful feeling, the survivor's renewed invulnerability, may itself have a counterproductive, boomerang effect—driving her to imagine she will remain in the clear also in future.

So, we will have survived safe and healthy, immune and immunized, perhaps already vaccinated, ever more protected and insured, fighting to be indemnified and beyond harm. We will celebrate a certain "resistance," leaving a fuzzy boundary between political struggle and an immunitarian ability to react. We won't be able to consider ourselves veterans or survivors of a conflict—for while military vocabulary has dominated the media narrative, we know that this was no war. To imagine what happened in these terms would be a repeat error, an obstacle to any reflection. This was not a war—no one has won. Many were overwhelmed without being able to put up a fight. Many lost everything, from integrity to property—and they were the very people who owned less than others, the most exposed and most defenseless.

If we have emerged unscathed from this enormous, unprecedented catastrophe of breathing, this is not cause to imagine that we are untouchable, beyond harm's reach. If we are in the clear, that does not mean we are now saved. Rather than a final success, immunity turns into its very opposite, like when the cure turns out be poisonous. Thus, the attempt to avoid harm at all costs, to calculate the incalculable, to set up hyper-defenses, all ends up in failure. The organism that sends out its troops of antibodies in order to block access to the foreign antigens risks destroying itself precisely in its attempt to protect its own invulnerability. This is what the autoimmune diseases show us. So, it is necessary to protect ourselves from protection and from the phantom of an absolute immunization.

Breathing has always been the symbol, the metonym, the marker of existence. To exist is to breathe. There is nothing more natural, more emblematic. Yet, already at the beginning of the last century, breathing was systematically targeted. We need only think of the ever wider and more sophisticated use of gases and poisons: from chlorine on the front lines of war, to the use of cyanide acid for extermination; and from radioactive contamination to chemical weapons. And it would seem that the science of toxic clouds and the theory of unbreathable spaces would continue to make progress even after this. This is true to the point that we could even speak—as Peter Sloterdijk has suggested—of "atmoterrorism." For what is now targeted is not a designated victim but rather the atmosphere in which they live. No longer is there direct blame or clear responsibility. Those who die are cut down by their own impulse to breath. Who, then, is to blame? The manipulation of the air has put an end to the naive privilege enjoyed by human beings before the caesura that was the twentieth century: namely, the privilege of breathing without worrying about the atmosphere surrounding them.

It is no accident that literature watched this with such apprehension. Hermann Broch offered the insight that breathing would no longer be nature—he diagnosed that, once air had ended up becoming a battlefield, the human community would be suffocated by the poisons deployed against itself. This internally directed atmoterrorism was already showing suicidal characteristics. In his essay *The Meridian* Paul Celan celebrated breathing—and denounced how it was being exterminated. He captured and articulated the wheezing of the victims; and he promoted their redemption, in the poem he called the "breathturn."

No one could have imagined this catastrophe of breathing, prompted by a virus that nonetheless seems to stand out against the backdrop of a troubling continuity. The air had lost its innocence for some time already. And, after the greenhouse effect, the breath of existence is no longer free or natural. Disorientation, the loss of a sense of place, means this, too—that an atmosphere pervaded by microbe competitors is unbreathable and uninhabitable. But there is no option other than to coexist. And this is the context in which the new sciences are discovering immune systems.

Distrust grows and suspicion increases. Unless we resort to vacuum-packed spaces, we will have to live in a contaminated, infected, poisoned atmosphere. Integrity is a mirage that now lies in the past.

If the organism is to have acceptable conditions, it must devote itself to a permanent watchfulness, an insomniac surveillance. Viruses and bacteria are among us. These new and aggressive co-occupants invade even intimacy itself, besieging this ancient abode and trying to settle here. The hygiene society makes its call to arms and immunity becomes an ideology. Obsessive self-care and continual medicalization are the mirror of a selective closedness, of a convinced refusal of participation, of an obstinate conservationism. The immune systems are security services specialized in protection and defense against invisible invaders, migrant viruses with the gall to occupy the same biological space. The mirage of immunity proceeds hand in glove with globalization.

These are not only allusive metaphors. The elevation of immunity extends far beyond biochemical or medical categories. Indeed, it is no accident that the most recent philosophy, starting with Jacques Derrida, has reflected on this. For it shows evident political, juridical, religious and psychological characteristics.

In the epidemic world, biopolitics has not lost value and relevance, but rather becomes yet stronger, becoming immunopolitics. The latent catastrophe coursing through and troubling the early decades of the new century is not, however, a simple danger on the horizon, such as could be captured within some governmental risk calculation. We must not minimize its importance or play down its intensity or reach. The catastrophe is ungovernable and brings to light all the limits of neoliberal governance. It is an interruption that marks the course of history, makes a dent on existence, changes habitats, habitants, inhabitation and cohabitation. It has the tone of the irreversible and the timbre of the irreparable. Nothing will be like it was before. Yesterday's world appears as a remote, collapsed world that has now slipped away. In the unpoetic and mournful present, breathing has been set into disarray.

But rather than lumber in a catastrophic relationship with catastrophe, what is instead needed is to consider the demand that the global pandemic has highlighted. The fight playing out between the virus and antibodies in the human organism is no border dispute. For the self and the stranger are bound up in an intricate game. The immune system, intervening with its flying squads and its security troops, risks going too far. In the attempt to eliminate the other, the self ends up killing itself or exposing itself to autoimmune diseases. The identitarian, sovereigntist self does not come out of this well. This, also because it presumes an integrity that does not in fact exist; for micro-clashes and little guerrillas are always popping up within. The so-called "infective dose" is indispensable. If the antibodies are to work, they have to play the part of strangers, and not vaunt their indigenous pride. In that role—and theater can help, here!—they must recognize themselves as resident foreigners. This will bring salvation—and health. Police-type defenses are no help even here.

We will have to live alongside this virus and perhaps with others. That means cohabiting with the rest of life, in complex, overlapping, intersecting environments. This must take place under the sign of a shared vulnerability—and this vulnerability is what has now been rediscovered.

ABOUT THE AUTHOR

Donatella Di Cesare teaches theoretical philosophy at the Sapienza University in Rome. One of the most significant voices on the Italian intellectual scene, she is an authoritative contributor to numerous newspapers, websites and journals in Italy and elsewhere. Her books have been translated into eight languages.